Reading to, with, and by Children

Reading to, with, and by Children

Margaret E. Mooney

Richard C. Owen Publishers, Inc.
Katonah, New York

Library of Congress Cataloging-in-Publication Data

Mooney, Margaret E.
    Reading to, with, and by children / Margaret E. Mooney.
        p.   cm.
    ISBN 0-913461-18-0
    1. Reading—Language experience approach.   2. Children—Books and
reading.   3. Reading (Primary)—New Zealand.   I. Title.
LB1050.35.M66   1990
372.4—dc20   90-30678
                                                                  CIP

RICHARD C. OWEN PUBLISHERS, INC.
PO Box 585
Katonah, New York 10536

Printed in the United States of America

Book design by Ken Venezio

ı

Table of Contents

Reading to, with, and by Children

1

Introduction

This book is based on my New Zealand experience as a teacher, consultant, editor, and educator. That experience has been questioned, confirmed, and extended through several periods of working in other South Pacific countries and in the United States. However, my New Zealand experience is not unique. It reflects the events of many classrooms at all grade levels throughout the world.

In New Zealand a reading program is not limited to any package, or series of materials, or set of teaching steps. "Program" means everything that is planned for and happens in a school or classroom: the philosophy; the way it is implemented; the resources; and the management of time, people, resources, and space. New Zealand teachers do not restrict their reading programs to one set of materials, but all material used reflects one set of principles. Although the examples in this book are from the Ready to Read series, developed and distributed to all New Zealand schools by the Department of Education for use as a core series in the first three years at school, the principles are relevant to any material which reflects children's ideas and experiences at any level of a school system.

This book is intended to help teachers make informed decisions about the learning opportunities they offer the children, and to ensure that children find reading an enjoyable and successful experience.

WHAT IS READING?

There are as many definitions of reading as there are readers, and that is as it should be. Reading is a personal experience. Each person's expectations, satisfactions, and responses not only differ from those of others but vary from experience to experience. Reading is a reflection and a refinement of one's understandings about life, both as it is perceived and lived. Any book on reading reflects the author's view, but that view will be modified according to each reader's experience and understandings.

Reading is the sharing of meaning. It is interaction between the giver and the receiver. Reading is the creation and recreation of meaning; and it takes place through the nonverbal as well as verbal modes of language—through listening and speaking, reading and writing, moving and watching, shaping and viewing. Reading is not merely a curriculum subject able to be confined to any one period, for reading is part of any exchange of meaning through text. However, most teachers do find they need to focus specifically on reading and related experiences for some part of each school day. This book is based on the premise that what happens during reading time is affected by and affects everything that happens during the entire school day. It also affects children's views of themselves and their world.

All power to those who have the privilege of helping children develop their view of reading!

2

Learning to Talk and Learning to Read

It is not coincidental that many of the books published in recent years on the teaching of reading have included at least one chapter on links between the way in which children learn to talk and in which they learn to read and write. In recent years research, observation, and experience have established and proved that the conditions and attitudes which nurture the acquisition of speech also foster the development of competence and confidence as children become readers and writers. Before trying to replicate these conditions and attitudes within the school environment and program, the reasons, as well as the implications of their implementation, need to be considered.

LEARNING TO TALK

Children learn to talk because they see and hear talk in action. They see how people use talk in their daily lives, and how talk enables them to get what they want and to enjoy being with others.

Children are surrounded by talk as their families work, eat, and play together. The children gradually begin to realize that all talk is not the same, and that people respond to talk in different ways. They become aware of the patterns and rhythms of talk, and of the variety of length, tone, and pace people use in talk.

As more and more of the talk is directed to them, children realize that they are expected to respond. They do this first as babies by cooing and then babbling, and the delight of hearing and feeling themselves talk and seeing the response it gets, encourages them to babble and coo more. The family accepts these noises as talk, and responds by talking to and with the children more frequently about more things for longer spans of time. They fill in the meaning of what they think the children are saying and talk more about it, repeating and extending what has been said or saying it another way. This provides further models for the children to practice and use. The babbles and coos become messages of more meaning and then larger chunks of meaning. The family and community continue to accept and respond to children's efforts and encourage more practice and development through more extensive and complex conversation.

All of this happens naturally and as part of normal living. There is no set time or sequence for learning to talk. Children do not have to learn one set of sentences before they learn the next. They are considered to be talkers, and makers and receivers of meaning through talk, right from the beginning. Listeners amend their responses according to what they know the children intended them to hear and to what they know they can do. It's a supportive exchange where each child's learning rate is accepted without question or overt concern. It is expected that every child will be able to talk. And it is accepted that this learning will not take place at any one moment or in any one way or even follow any set pattern.

Children learn to talk as they live and work and play. It's through living and talking with others that they discover what talk can do for them. They learn how to get what they need, how to share their ideas and feelings, and how to find out more about the world.

Children learn to talk by:

being surrounded by people talking.
people talking to them.
talking with others.
talking by themselves and to others.

LEARNING TO READ

Children learn to read in the same way. They learn to read by:

seeing and hearing others read.
listening to others read to them.

reading with others.

reading by themselves and to others.

Children learn to read by being surrounded by talk and print. They see how the printed word gives messages to the reader. As they listen to others read to them, children realize that the printed word can be used to tell new stories and bring new meanings to their lives. They learn that many of the events and ideas they hear read to them are similar to those they have experienced and reflect the way they feel about their experiences.

As children hear more and more stories, and as they become aware of people reading and responding to print, they are motivated to do likewise. They want to get their own messages and meanings from labels, notices, books, and signs. There will be no set order or way in which this will happen. Children will be spurred on to greater effort and achievement through plenty of support and encouragement in the same way they were given support when they learned to talk, as well as through continued demonstrations and sharing.

Reading "Nearly Right"

Children need adults to respond to these efforts in total, rather than always demanding accurate detail and structure. The children's "mistakes" should be seen as "nearly rights" in the same way as they were when the children were learning to talk. In this way children see that the exchange of meaning is what is as important in reading and writing as it is in talking. Continued encouragement and support, and the provision of further models through stories, rhymes, and songs will help children develop strategies for coping with difficulties and increasing accuracy and independence.

These attitudes, understandings, and behaviors children develop as they learn to talk affect the meanings children acquire and the way in which they create and recreate them as they learn to read and write. Children will be helped to learn to read and write as successfully and as naturally as they learned to talk if they experience a program which includes:

talking to children.
talking with children.
talking by children.

reading to children.
reading with children.
reading by children.

writing to and for children.
writing with children.
writing by children.

Some of the approaches used to provide these experiences are reading to children, shared reading, language experience, guided reading, and independent reading. Detailed discussion of each of these approaches forms the bulk of this book, but an overview here will provide a base for comparative reading of those chapters.

Reading to Children

Reading to children widens their horizons and understandings about books, their experiences, and their world. The teacher acts as the author and the reader presenting a variety of forms and styles of writing, enabling children to understand that the written word has meaning and that the meaning is accessible through the act of reading.

Children are able to enjoy the author's ideas through an aural and usually, but not necessarily, visual experience. They do not have to concentrate on, or take responsibility for, the mechanics of gaining meaning from the printed word. They see a reader reading and are able to experience the satisfactions and delights of the product of reading— meaning. This establishes a desire to be readers themselves through emulating the successful model of the teacher reading to children.

Shared Reading

Shared reading is an approach where the teacher replicates the bedtime story situation with the class, a group of children, or an individual child to enable them to enjoy and participate in the reading of books which they cannot yet read for themselves. The emphasis is on the enjoyment of the story as a whole; and any participation by the child or children is motivated more often by the story line and the story's structure than by any direction from the teacher. Invitations from the teacher are to "read along with" rather than to take responsibility for being the main reader.

Language-experience Approach

The language-experience approach is a combination of writing to and for children, and reading to, with, and by them. Traditionally it has been linked with experiences designed specifically for recording on a wall-story or chart.

Any experience or thought can form the basis of a language experience, with the child or children seeing how their ideas can be recorded and then revisited by them or by others. Language experience emphasizes the importance of content of immediate relevance and accessibility to the children—principles of any whole-language program.

Guided Reading

In guided reading the teacher and a group of children, or sometimes an individual child, talk and think and question their way through a book of which they each have a copy. The teacher shows the children what questions to ask of themselves as readers, and of the author through the text, so that each child can discover the author's meaning on the first reading. Guided reading is dependent on the teacher being aware of each child's competencies, interests, and experiences; being able to determine the supports and challenges offered by a book; and accepting the role of supporting learning rather than directing teaching.

Independent Reading

In independent reading the children assume full responsibility for reading, expecting to be able to overcome any challenges or to know where to get any necessary help. Independent reading is not a stage to be reached, but is part of every stage of development. It confirms oneself as a reader through taking responsibility for exploring new books, as well as revisiting known ones. Independent reading should be a successful and self-motivated part of every reader's day, for an independent reader is one who not only knows how to read but chooses to read and knows how to make time to do so.

Figure 2.1 shows the links between reading to children, reading with children, and reading by children, and the main approaches in a whole-language program. It also shows the comparative amounts of support and responsibility in each approach.

Figure 2.1
Links in Reading

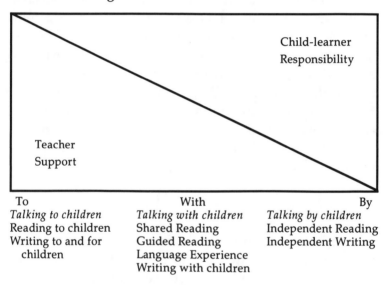

To	With	By
Talking to children	*Talking with children*	*Talking by children*
Reading to children	Shared Reading	Independent Reading
Writing to and for children	Guided Reading	Independent Writing
	Language Experience	
	Writing with children	

The figure illustrates the cyclical nature of learning and the independence which is part of every developmental stage. The diagonal line shows the amount of support needed by the learner over time.

3

Focusing on the Reader

When children are learning to talk, adults focus on what children can already say. They concern themselves with ways in which that learning can be confirmed and extended. Adults know what opportunities and support to provide and how to react to children's responses because they are aware of what learning has already taken place and how it has happened. "Needs" do not become a major concern, and comparisons between children are not made to reveal failures or deficiencies or to confirm that reteaching or remediation is required. The children are given additional support and encouragement and their efforts receive greater focus and praise. New models and expectations arise from achievements.

CONTINUATION OF READING

And so it should be with learning to read. A program which focuses on children and their continued learning and development as readers requires acceptance of learning and teaching as positive and continuous and not compensatory processes. The competencies already in place are the starting points for further learning. Evaluation and planning are synonymous, both in attitude and action.

As with helping children to learn to talk the rhythm of developing readers and writers is not teach and test and then reteach or new teaching and more testing. The most effective rhythm is continuous and simultaneous interacting, observing, modeling, interacting, responding, and encouraging. And the focus is always on the learners—what they do, how they do and show it, and what they are striving to do; on what attitudes, understandings, and behaviors they display.

Traditionally teachers have centered their evaluation of children's progress or a program on the skills necessary to complete predetermined exercises or tests. While skills are necessary tools for reading, they are well down the process line. In a whole-language context skills are behaviors which are the product or manifestation of attitudes and understandings. A skill can only be considered part of the reader's repertoire when the reader knows how to decide that it is the most efficient and appropriate means of achieving the desired result. The reason for choosing to do something in a particular way and being aware of the result is a prerequisite for using any skill.

Skills can only be acquired, understood, and used in

the course of real reading. Whatever the stage of a reader's development, skills are interdependent. No one skill can be learned, used, or evaluated in isolation. Beginning readers picking up a one-sentence-per-page book with an exact text-picture match use exactly the same process to get meaning as you would use when reading the latest issue of your favorite magazine. The degree to which skills are consciously used and the amount of attention to print and illustration will differ, but the process will be the same.

Readers refine and use skills more efficiently and automatically every time they read for and with meaning.

STAGES OF READING

The attitudes, understandings, and behaviors readers display reflect their general stage of reading development and can be grouped into three broad stages—emergent, early, and fluency.

The emergent, or starting, stage emphasizes enjoyment and enrichment. Books can be shared again and again, providing children with further explorations of the text and for further innovation and extension leading to independent reading. Even before children can read by themselves they can appreciate literature, become familiar with patterns of language in books, and can also become aware that books have special conventions that point up the author's message. Children learn that text, as well as illustrations, give meaning to the reader. As children are guided to read with the teacher's help they also learn what will happen next in the story line.

In the early reading stage, as children are becoming readers, they and the teacher discuss the background of the story so that the plot and theme become clear. At this stage readers learn to pay close attention to the structure and meaning of sentences. The habit of reading for meaning, of taking risks and making approximations, of predicting and confirming the use of letter-sound associations, of self-correcting, and of rerunning and reading on when meaning has been lost is established.

In the fluency stage, when children are reading by themselves, teachers emphasize the development of children's competence and confidence in integrating cues; maintaining meaning through longer, more complex structures; and adjusting reading rate with the purpose of reading.

Further explanations of these three stages can be found in *Developing Life-long Readers,* [1] where the attitudes, understandings, and behaviors most commonly displayed at each stage are discussed.

The groupings are not clear cut. At any one time each reader will show competence in different aspects. The competencies will change from time to time and will not be confined to only one level. The characteristics are not definitive or exhaustive, and should not be considered as a checklist. A responsive teacher will be aware of and watchful for verbal and nonverbal displays of each reader's reactions to his or her own efforts as readers and writers and to those of others. These insights will help teachers to select appropriate material and present it for readers' satisfaction and enjoyment.

[1] Mooney, Margaret. *Developing Life-long Readers.* Wellington, New Zealand: Department of Education, 1988. Pages 8–9. Distributed in the United States by Richard C. Owen Publishers, Inc.

4

Choosing the Appropriate Approach

The decision about which approach—shared reading, language experience, guided reading, or independent reading—should be used with any one book and a group of children is the teacher's responsibility, or the teacher's and the children's. The teacher's decision will be based on:

- the understandings, experiences, attitudes, and expectations the children bring to the reading.
- the children's competencies as readers and writers.
- the ratio between supportive features and challenges presented in the concepts, structures, language, illustrations, and layout of the book.

- the amount and type of support the teacher will be required to give in order that the children interact with the author's ideas.
- the purpose of the reading.

The teacher will be able to select any approach only as a starting point. The responses from the children, and the help they seek and need at any stage within the lesson, will dictate the approach most suitable for that part of the reading. The switch from one approach to another should be as unobtrusive as possible, and should not interrupt the flow of the story. During the reading the teacher should adjust his or her input according to the children's contributions and responses. The greater the participation by children, the less the teacher should overtly contribute. The teacher must be alert to his or her role, as well as that of the reader and the author. Whatever approach is used, it should be seen as a means of making meaning accessible to the children and of developing self-motivated and independent readers.

USING EACH APPROACH

Each approach should be included in the daily classroom program at every level of the elementary school. The amount of time spent on any one approach will vary from child to child, group to group, grade to grade, and, within any one class, from day to day and lesson to lesson. During the first weeks of the school year it is likely that there will be more reading to, shared reading, and language experience than guided or independent reading. The first three approaches enable the teacher to get to know children's interests, abilities, and experiences without expecting the children to take responsibilities beyond their capabilities. These approaches also provide opportunities for children to work together as a cohesive and supportive group. When more guided and independent reading are introduced to the program the children will feel confident in making a greater contribution and taking more responsibility. They will feel supported as they take risks in their own reading, and will be supportive to the ideas and efforts of others.

It is also true that in a kindergarten room there will be more reading to, shared reading, and language experience than guided or independent reading. In reading to and shared reading, and in group language experiences, the amount and nature of support offered by the teacher and the other children enables each child to develop confidence and competence before taking on more responsibility for the first reading as required in guided or independent reading. In the higher grades there may be more guided and independent reading than there are of the other approaches.

However, all approaches have a place at every level of the school within each day and, usually, within each lesson. In a balanced program the approaches will be so intertwined that the children will move easily from one approach to another without commenting or even being aware of the change.

5

Reading to Children

Reading to children enables the teacher to demonstrate the nature, pleasures, and rewards of reading, and to increase children's interest in books and their desire to be readers.

When children have frequent opportunities to hear stories, poems, rhymes, and chants read and sung to them, they become familiar with the ways in which language can be recorded, and they learn how stories work. Children realize that some of their experiences and thoughts are similar to those that have been recorded by authors. Hearing them from another perspective adds new meaning and impact to children's own thoughts and experiences.

Children also become aware that their memories, under-standings, and past experiences help them to recreate those presented in the writings of others. As children become familiar with ideas, events, and feelings through being read to, they make their own narratives in their heads and want to create and record their own texts. Thus children are moti-vated to be readers and writers.

HOW STORIES WORK

When children have frequent opportunities to hear texts written by others, and to relate those writings to their own experiences, they can practice composing stories in their heads. They are refining the understandings they already have about patterns, sounds, rhythms, and styles of lan-guage. Listening to known stories allows children to con-firm their predictions about how the episodes are strung together to make the story work, and the ways in which the ideas will be presented. Children will also discover new levels of meaning. This enables them to extend and refine their own texts. In the early stages of reading development this familiarity establishes an expectation that what is read will make sense. Thus children see reading and writing as part of the same meaning-driven process. Familiarity with knowing how stories work helps beginning readers develop confidence in becoming involved in the unfolding of the story line when they hear new stories or assume more of the reader's role for themselves.

As children move through the stages of reading develop-ment this refining and extending of meaning through aural experiences enables them to practice editing their own "in-the-head" stories, as well as those they record. It also provides a pattern for their continuing development in the process of predicting, sampling, and confirming text as they become more independent and extensive readers.

TEACHERS AS MODELS

The teacher's demonstration as a reader and writer at work provides models which children can approximate and refine according to their own stages of development as readers and writers. The pleasures and benefits of being read to are not the perogative of beginning readers. Readers at all levels need to have their horizons extended through enjoying material beyond their independent reading level or through aural and visual experiences. *Is this not one of the reasons why adults go to the theater?*

Children at all stages need constant demonstrations from teachers showing they value books and enjoy being readers and writers. Such demonstrations should not be confined to the language period. Reading and writing should be promoted and enjoyed as worthwhile activities at all times of the day and their place in other curriculum areas highlighted. When children are shown how to make time for enjoying and using books, they will not only consider reading a pleasurable option and an essential part of their daily lives but they will learn how to make time to read.

The relevance of reading and writing as an integrated part of a day's normal activity and not as separate subjects can be reinforced by introducing children to books and texts of all types and forms covering a wide range of content appropriate for children's interest and conceptual level.

Reading a variety of labels, poems, recipes, diaries, letters, stories, articles, and rhymes will show children how reading goes well beyond any lesson or school day.

TEACHER'S ATTITUDE TO READING

The teacher's attitude is important whatever the approach, but "selling" books through attitude is an important aspect of reading to children. Reading needs to be shown as an active and satisfying option which brings its own rewards. The teacher is the voice of the reader, the listener, and the author, showing children how to assume these roles with enthusiasm. Children need to feel in partnership with the teacher so they will be motivated to take an even greater role in the creation of their own texts and in recreating those of others.

6

Shared Reading

The shared reading of carefully selected material provides special opportunities for convincing children that they can be readers and writers, and for encouraging them to read and write in a supportive and success-oriented climate. The teacher can show children that as they become involved and participate in the story, they are co-readers with the teacher and co-writers with the author. The teacher accepts all approximations as children opt in and out of the reading. As the story line draws the children in, and they feel their efforts are accepted by the teacher and their peers, they increase their involvement and take a more active part in the reading.

Invitations to participate should come from the book itself and the way in which the teacher reads it, rather than by any planned or overt directions. For example, when children seem eager to join in, a nod or a smile or a pause so they can offer their predictions or comments will acknowledge their efforts and encourage more participation. The teacher could encourage more children to join in a repetitive or cumulative story by exaggerating the rhythm and nodding so children know their participation is invited and welcomed. On subsequent readings the invitations can be more obvious, with raised intonation sometimes indicating parts where the teacher thinks children would feel comfortable contributing.

The children's contributions may range from reading in their heads or mouthing some of the words to an enthusiastic rendering, which will probably include a number of approximations. All efforts should be encouraged and accepted, with teachers being mindful that shared reading is more about inviting children to act as readers and writers and enjoy the story as a whole than accumulating a long list of words named accurately.

BOOKS THAT INTEREST CHILDREN

If children are to be drawn into the reading by the books, teachers need to provide materials that have immediate interest for the reader and a strong story line with an accessible structure. Such books aid the development of predictive strategies within the reader as they seek to unfold meaning. Many whole-language enthusiasts advocate "predictable books" as essential materials, with rhyme, rhythm, and repetition seen as key features of these books. It is suggested that these characteristics, or those contained in "predictable books," do not necessarily, or alone, make a book suitable for beginning readers. The focus must be on ways in which the author encourages readers to feel as if their hands are also on the author's pen, confident of the direction the story is most likely to follow. Suggested criteria for the selection of material suitable for use in shared reading and other approaches include the appeal of the book to the child, the worth of the idea, the appropriateness of the story's shape and structure, the effectiveness of the language, the authenticity of the story, the help illustrations give readers in gaining meaning, and the appropriateness of the book's format. Further discussion of book selection criteria can be found in *Developing Life-long Readers.*[1] These criteria were used for the selection of scripts now published in the Ready to Read series, the national reading books used in all New Zealand classrooms for children in their first years of school. However, the criteria are applicable to materials at all levels.

A teacher can use the shared reading approach with an individual child or with a group of children, which may be part or all of the class. Whatever organization is used, the emphasis of all shared readings should be each child's personal enjoyment of the story in its entirety. Any readings for attention to details of vocabulary, structure, grammar, or any other specifics should not interfere with that pleasure or with the child-author interaction.

---

[1] Mooney, Margaret. *Developing Life-long Readers.* Wellington, New Zealand: Department of Education, 1988. Pages 4–5. Distributed in the United States by Richard C. Owen Publishers, Inc.

Right from the beginning children need to understand that readers read to find out what the author is saying, and that words are only a means to that end. Readers do not read in order to acquire or practice using a root word or initial letter or cloze procedure. Attention to any print details or conventions should be within the context of the whole story, and only brought into focus to resolve a real difficulty encountered in the text. In shared reading such attention would only occur after the children have the story's idea and shape in their heads from the first or any previous readings.

Children should not feel that any reading has been initiated for the prime purpose of acquiring a particular skill or vocabulary item. If they do, the children will soon consider reading as an exercise done in order to earn praise for correct answers; and the desire to please the teacher will, in time, kill the desire to read for reading's sake. This is particularly so when an enlarged text is used, making it easier for the teacher to focus the attention of a number of children on the print.

"BIG BOOKS"

Enlarged-text books are a wonderful resource, but it is not necessary to have a "big book" for shared reading, especially a first reading when the focus is on the idea of the story and interaction with and through that. Any sized book or material can be used for shared reading.

A book, whatever its size or shape, is only a vehicle, not an approach. A good book can be used in any approach, and this applies to enlarged texts or "big books." No approach is dependent on any one book format. The approach is the amount and nature of support the teacher gives, and the amount of responsibility the reader takes.

The aim of an enlarged text is to lead children back to the regular-sized publication which can be read wherever and whenever a child wishes. A five-year-old would find it very difficult to curl up in bed with a big book. However, sometimes a teacher finds it very difficult to draw the attention of a group of children to textual or illustrative details in a regular-sized book. There is a place for both formats, but the format does not drive the approach.

The benefits of shared reading can be extended when teachers and children choose to make their own "big book" in response to a story or text. Making a book enables the teacher to model some of the ways in which an author's ideas can be revisited and related to one's own experiences in more detail than can be assimilated on the first reading of a story. For example, after becoming familiar with *The Biggest Cake in the World*[2] children could make an enlarged book for further shared, guided, or independent reading about the biggest pizza in the world or the biggest traffic jam in New York. The structure and the shape of the story can provide a framework for their ideas. Or children could write about and illustrate the biggest thing they have ever seen.

Making a book is only one way of responding to a book, and teachers will need to explore other possibilities with the children, accepting as many of their suggestions as practical. This topic is discussed further in Chapter 11.

---

[2] Cowley, Joy. *The Biggest Cake in the World,* in Ready to Read series. Wellington, New Zealand: Department of Education, 1983. Distributed in the United States by Richard C. Owen Publishers, Inc.

SHARED READING

The shared reading approach can be used with groups of varying numbers, ages, and abilities, as well as with individual children. Children should not associate the approach with massed reading in which they are just one of a group. Personal satisfaction from and enjoyment of the story, as well as the conviction that reading is worthwhile and that it is for them personally, should be the long-term effect of any shared reading experience. In the shared reading of any book children should feel they will be supported until they become so familiar with the story and how it works that they will be able to read it successfully for themselves.

Sample Lesson: Shared Reading at The Emergent Stage[1]

T SHIRTS[2]

This book is suitable for shared reading at the emergent stage where children are developing understandings about the constancy of print, print conventions, and how books work, and are working toward a word-voice-finger match.

T shirts are universal clothing, so most, if not all, children will be able to identify immediately with the theme. And the characters will provide another "known" element. The clear illustrations provide the necessary cues, even if children cannot focus on the text. The story moves along at a good pace and has an inherent rhythm that will draw the children in to the reading.

The following suggestions will need to be adapted according to the experiences and understandings the teacher

---

[1] See Chapter 3 for a discussion of the emergent stage.
[2] Corney, Estelle. *T Shirts*, in Ready to Read series. Wellington, New Zealand: Department of Education, 1983. Distributed in the United States by Richard C. Owen Publishers, Inc.

knows the children bring to the reading and the way in which they respond to the book.

- Look at the cover. Can you tell me what this book is going to be about?
- How do you think T shirts got their name?
- Can you make your body look like a T shirt?
- What other letters can you make with your body?
- Who is wearing a T shirt today?
- What color is your T shirt?
- What's on your T shirt?
- Let's look at the T shirt on the cover of our book.
- These T shirts tell us the name of the book, who wrote the story, and who illustrated it.

The teacher points to the title, author's name, and that of the illustrator while reading the corresponding words.

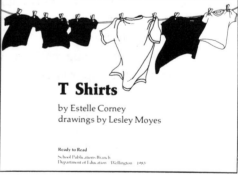

Title Page

- And here are the T shirts we're going to meet in the book.
- Here's the title of our story, and the author's name and the illustrator's, just as they were on the cover.

Pages 2–3

The teacher begins reading the story at a normal pace, but emphasizes the strong rhythm and pattern of the language and points to "ME" on the T shirt at the appropriate time.

- I wonder who will be wearing the next T shirt?

I've got a T shirt,
A yellow, yellow T shirt,
And on my yellow T shirt
There's a great big ME.

Pages 4–5

The teacher continues the reading, pausing before "orange" and "HE," indicating an invitation to the children to predict and, perhaps, participate.

- Who will be next?
- Watch and see if you are right.

Pages 6–9

Invitations to participate should not interrupt the flow of the reading. However, it is likely that even on the first reading children will be reading along with the teacher. The strong rhythm, repetitive pattern, clear and supportive illustrations, the natural development of the story line, and the questioning skill of the teacher will draw the children in and they will be eager to contribute.

Dad's got a T shirt,
A big orange T shirt,
And on his orange T shirt
There's a great big HE.

Pages 10–11

On this first reading it is likely that most of the children will not participate to the same degree as with books they have read previously—until the last two lines. This should not slow the teacher's pace or be taken as an indication that "teaching" is required. Increased familiarity through subsequent readings will soon enable the children to read along confidently and successfully.

It is very likely that the children will ask that the book be read again immediately. If not, the teacher could say: Would you like me to read that again?

Before commencing the second reading the teacher could say: You know how the story works now, so you will be able to read along with me and join in more of the story.

Page turnings could be preceded by: Can you remember who we will meet now? What will be on the T shirt?

Mum's got a T shirt,
A big purple T shirt,

And on her purple T shirt
There's a great big SHE.

As with all questions during the reading the answers need not be vocalized. The function of these questions is to show the reader what to ask of the book and how to control the unfolding of the story line.

Before the lesson ends or moves to another part children could be reminded that the book is available for them to read: I'll put the book on the "Favorite Book" shelf in the book corner. You might like to read it again by yourself or with a friend.

Later in the day the teacher or a child may initiate another shared reading of the book. Each reading will increase the children's participation; and the teacher will soon be able to be one of the readers instead of taking the lead. If the response to the suggestion of another reading is not enthusiastic the book should not be pursued further.

This book has proved to be a winner, but not all books will be. Every shared reading should be enjoyable. Books which prove they hold no further appeal for a particular group of children should not be pursued any further. No

My brothers all have T shirts,
Little red T shirts,
And on their little T shirts
They have ONE, TWO, THREE.

book, no matter how good, should be over done. Children should always feel there is going to be some new discovery at each reading.

As *T Shirts* will probably be used for shared reading with children during their first weeks at school the teacher should spend some time introducing and exploring some of the responses that could be made. The degree to which this would be appropriate will be determined by the children's enthusiasm for the book: We could use the pattern of this story to make up our own stories about T shirts or about the T shirts we are wearing.

This could be said, and then a book or wall-story made for further shared reading. Or the teacher could write the pattern on the blackboard or chalkboard or on a card with lift-up sections for the parts which will vary.

Now we've washed the T shirts,
The big and little T shirts,
And, hanging on the line,
In the wind, we see . . .

ONE, TWO, THREE,
HE, SHE, ME.

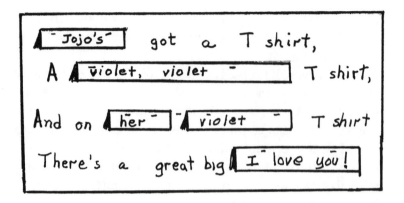

- Let's write another story about Jojo's shirt.
- What could I change to make a new story?
- What color is Jojo's shirt?
- Where will we put that?
- What's written on Jojo's shirt?
- Where does that go in our story?
- Let's read our story about Jojo's shirt.

Two or three examples would be sufficient. Other versions could be added later, perhaps by individual children. The card could be used for shared reading during the "tuning-in" or community session at the beginning of the language period or at breaks in the day. It would be ideal for independent reading by individuals or groups of children. A pointer could be provided, allowing children to match the spoken and written words in a tactile way. The rhythm of *T Shirts* provides support for children trying to establish this one-to-one matching, and each section provides a manageable amount of text.

Children could use the structure of the book to write about different items of clothing or their belongings. Their writing could be shared with other children, displayed in the classroom, or added to the book corner resources.

Children could make their own paper T shirts and hang these on a line across the room.

Children's responses will dictate whether or not it would be appropriate to extend the book's stimulus. There should always be enough excitement and interest left in the original publication for children to want to read it on their own.

7

Language Experience

Language experience enables the teacher to help children explore, record, consider, read about, and share their experiences, feelings, and ideas through talking, reading, and writing. The teacher can record children's language and provide opportunities for writing to be shared through the other "to, with, and by" approaches to reading. The language-experience approach can be used with individual children or with a group or class. The aim of the approach is to help children develop these understandings:

- I can talk about what happens to me, how I feel, and what I think about.

- My talk can be written down, either by me or by someone else.
- I can read what is written down because it is my story and I know how it is going to work and what it will say.
- Others can read my story or I can read it to them.

TEACHER'S ROLE

The teacher's role in language experience is to encourage children to talk about an experience or idea, to clarify what the children want recorded, and to ensure that what is written can be read and understood by others. A sensitive teacher can extend children's language and understanding of the experience or idea by showing children how to reflect on their feelings or memories or explore them in other ways. This can be done by acknowledging the children's efforts to express themselves, and sometimes by asking questions or making comments which will encourage further exploration or reflection by the children. These questions could include:

- Tell me more about . . .
- What did it remind you of?
- Did you see . . . ?
- How did you feel about that?
- Have you ever felt like that before?
- I'm sure you must have . . .
- I'm sure others would be interested to find out more about . . .

Sometimes confirming comments can be used to lead the children to rephrase or add to their stories. It is important that the teacher's verbal and nonverbal responses show children that it is their ideas and expressions which are valued and will be recorded and shared; and that ownership of the experience, feelings, and ideas, as well as the way in which they are recorded, belongs to them.

Children's stories can be recorded in a variety of ways, including topic books, single-title books, collections by individual children, wall-stories, diaries, charts, poems, songs, labels for models, or illustrations, letters, and journals. If children are to be able to record their own stories in a variety of ways and make choices about the one most appropriate for a particular topic or purpose, they need to see their ideas presented in different forms. Being involved in the creation of these models, as in language experience, provides strong motivation for independent writing.

WORKING WITH CHILDREN

Language experience provides unique opportunities for the teacher to work alongside the children as they relive and reconsider things of importance to them. Their cultural understandings will frame the way in which happenings or feelings are expressed; and teachers need to be aware of making each child feel comfortable in contributing to the discussion and participating in the recording and sharing. Children will then feel confident in writing about and with emotion; and they will see writing as a way of exploring their own feelings.

Teachers also need to consider the number of children involved in the discussion and sharing. Some language experiences are best kept within a small group, while others can be the motivation for exploration in other language modes or further talking, reading, and writing.

The most worthwhile sessions may well be those of an impromptu nature when the teacher responds to an unplanned moment or a sudden outburst of excitement, action, or concern. Teachers do not need to seek or stage special experiences in order that the language-experience approach be used.

8

Guided Reading

Through the approaches of reading to children and shared reading children are able to enjoy books that would present too many difficulties for them if they were to take responsibility for the first reading. In guided reading there is a careful match of text and children to ensure that each child in the group (usually six to eight children) is able to enjoy and control the story throughout the first reading. This means that the groups are relatively homogeneous. Although the children in any one group will reflect a range of competencies, experiences, and interests they will be working together at that particular time because the material offers each child a manageable amount of challenge. The groups will change as some children make faster or slower progress than others and it becomes obvious that they would benefit from working with another group. However, these changes would be from month to month rather than day to day.

Guided reading offers opportunities for the teacher to help children learn how to overcome these difficulties, without taking away the privilege of setting up their own dialogue with the author on the first reading of the text. Children learn what questions to ask of themselves as readers. They also learn to ask questions of, as well as find support in, the text, as they unfold and recreate the author's message as if they were creating it for the first time. In a sense each child is the author and the reader at the same time.

GUIDED READING VERSUS
TRADITIONAL METHODS

Guided reading is not a new name for instructional reading or any other form of group teaching or work with a basal. There are major differences in the intent and techniques between guided reading and the more traditional "teaching" methods. These differences need to be appreciated if guided reading is really to be "reading with and by children."

In guided reading the teacher uses questions and comments to help children become aware of resources within themselves and in the text which will enable them to overcome difficulties in that particular piece, as well as to meet similar challenges in other material. This is in direct contrast to techniques often employed in instructional reading and the methods advocated in the manuals of most basal series.

The teacher's role in these programs is to supply short-term help by focusing children's attention on the initial letter or some other specific textual detail, or by telling them the word without establishing any resource for overcoming similar challenges in subsequent reading. The traditional practice of instructional reading creates readers who become dependent on the teacher telling them what to do. They form the habit of appealing to the teacher for help when they meet a difficulty. When that help is not available or forthcoming they are unable to persevere with the reading.

The aim of guided reading is to develop independent readers who question, consider alternatives, and make informed choices as they seek meaning. Reading is an exploration and a discovery of themselves and their world through the author's message. Guided reading is an enabling and empowering approach where the focus is on the child as a long-term learner being shown how and why and which strategies to select and employ to ensure that meaning is gained and maintained during the reading and beyond. Attention to techniques only becomes a concern when meaning is lost, and then the emphasis is on the reader regaining meaning and continuing the reading, rather than interrupting it to learn and practice a particular skill. Teachers using the guided-reading approach know the supports and challenges a particular book will offer each child in the group; and they vary the amount and type of guidance they offer according to how each child is coping with the reading.

In the usual interpretation of instructional reading the teacher draws the children through a predetermined teaching sequence using a particular book to teach a specific skill. Any one or number of children in the group may not need to focus on that particular skill but may need support in using other coping strategies. However, teachers bound to a prescriptive manual or set teaching sequence have difficulty in accommodating such demands, and are unable to teach responsively as required when children are encouraged to be really reading the text.

Guided reading is based on the understanding that the children are the readers and they are the ones who must bring meaning to, and gain meaning from, the text as they read. The teacher is aware of the need for comprehension to be the act of engaging with, and responding to, meaning during the reading. Connections between the reader and the author are made as the reading unfolds, and are not dependent on the teacher being an interpreter or checker of meaning as in instructional reading.

READER'S ROLE

Guided reading requires the teacher to know what attitudes, understandings, and behaviors each child in the group will bring to the reading, as well as what supports and challenges are offered in the book. Children should not be introduced to guided reading until they have had plenty of opportunities to listen to a wide range of stories, poems, rhymes, and songs, and to join in shared reading experiences. They will then have some understandings of how books and stories work, and will be eager to take a more active part in reading the text themselves. They will be confident in their desire to be readers and to assume the reader's role.

The teacher will then be able to guide the children through any difficulties by following a skilled reader's sequence of:

- using context, experience, and knowledge of language and print to make informed guesses to unfold the text (*predicting*).
- attending to only those details of print necessary to confirm those expectations (*sampling*).
- checking that meaning has been maintained and that cross-references concur with the direction of the story line (*confirming*).
- employing other coping strategies where necessary to regain meaning (*self-correcting*).

For example, when helping an emergent reader experiencing difficulty with: *"Asleep" said the frog,* in *Old Tuatara,* [1] the teacher could say:

Look at the picture.
What do you think the words are going to tell you?
(*Predicting*).
Look at the text.
Read it with your eyes.
(*Sampling and confirming*).
Do you think you are right?
Does it make sense?
(*Cross-referencing and self-correcting*).

---

[1] Cowley, Joy. *Old Tuatara,* in Ready to Read series. Wellington, New Zealand: Department of Education, 1983. Distributed in the United States by Richard C. Owen Publishers, Inc.

"Asleep," said the frog.

How do you know?
(*Confirming*).
Would you like to read the sentence to me?

This example, and those following, show how the teacher raises appropriate questions in the children's minds, but does not expect a response until the readers have had time and support to think their way through the difficulty and feel confident of success. The examples also show how children are helped to use skills interdependently, thus integrating cues from a number of sources to predict as well as confirm that particular section of text within the whole

Mum hosed the car.
Mark and Helen cleaned
the windows and the doors.
Mum cleaned the roof.

This is the way we clean the car,
Clean the car, clean the car;
This is the way we clean the car,
On a Saturday morning.

context of the story. For example, a child reading at the early stage and having difficulty in *Saturday Morning*[2] with:

Mark and Helen cleaned
the windows and the doors.

could be supported as follows:

Leave the word out, read on, and think what would make sense.
(*Predicting using cloze through semantic and syntactic cues*).
Does that make sense?
(*Confirming*).

[2] *Saturday Morning,* in Ready to Read series. Wellington, New Zealand: Department of Education, 1983. Distributed in the United States by Richard C. Owen Publishers, Inc.

How do you know?
(*Cross-referencing and self-correcting*).
What does your word begin/end with?
(*Checking using graphophonic cues*).
Do you see that in the text?
(*Checking by cross-referencing*).
Read the sentence again.
(*Going back to the context, self-correcting if necessary, and continuing the reading*).

Or, a child at the fluency stage reading "Rosie Climbs the Sky Tree"[3] who is having difficulty with *and sure enough* in:

"I must think hard about what to do next."
Rosie thought hard,
and sure enough, she had an idea.

This child could be told:

Go back and read the previous sentence again.
(*Predicting using cloze through semantic and syntactic cues*).
Can you think what words or phrase might be used which would make sense?
Leave that phrase out and read on.
Now go back and read that part again.
(*Confirming and cross-checking*).
How did you check you were right?
(*Confirming*).

---

[3] Mahy, Margaret. "Rosie Climbs the Sky Tree," in *Dog Talk* pages 38–45. Ready to Read series. Wellington, New Zealand: Department of Education, 1988. Distributed in the United States by Richard C. Owen Publishers, Inc.

Did you notice . . . ? or Did you check?
(*Showing other possibilities for confirming*).

When children's reading development is observed in terms of attitudes, understandings, and behaviors the teacher is able to consider more than how well a skill has been taught and/or learned. Knowing a skill is different from knowing which combination of skills from an even wider repertoire will provide the most appropriate strategy for that particular reading, and being able to "change gears" if not successful. It's the "on-the-spot mix and match" from all available cues that allows readers to concentrate on their dialogue with the author.

READERS CONTROL READING

If the emphasis is on readers controlling their reading the teacher is able to observe objectively how children are operating, and identify what further learning opportunities are required to ensure the children's continued development. In this way planning and evaluation become an integral part of the program; the teacher is working from a positive viewpoint, responding to the things children do successfully. Known learning becomes the springboard within each child for further effort and learning. Observing children's attitudes to and understandings about reading, and their behavior when reading, reflects the multi-faceted nature of learning. It also enables the teacher to identify common competencies within the group, as well as those normally associated with children at a particular stage of development.

Competencies in some characteristics from more than one stage will be evident at any one time in any one child; and they will be seen in reading as well as in writing and other areas of learning. For example, a child who sees risk-taking as a part of striving toward gaining meaning during reading will probably also be making more self-corrections as cross-referencing and confirming become integrated and automatic strategies. At the same time the child may sometimes display behaviors associated with earlier stages of development; for example, finger pointing. When writing, the child may waver between trying to keep the flow of script closer to the flow of ideas than at other times. And there may be times when details are labored or the form repetitive through several pieces of writing.

The inter-relationship of attitudes, understandings, and behaviors at any one level, as well as between levels, can be seen in the following example. Emergent readers who expect to make sense of what is read to them and what they read (*attitude*) will understand the importance of background knowledge and will use this to get meaning (*understanding*). This will be reflected in the way they retell stories in sequence, predict events and episodes, and use pictures to anticipate the text (*behavior*).

At the early stage readers will expect to get meaning from the text; and they will be willing to work at this (*attitude*). They understand how real and imaginary experiences influence the meaning gained from the text (*understanding*); and this is reflected in the way they select and integrate appropriate strategies (*behavior*).

At the fluency stage readers expect to meet more challenges, especially in style, form, and specialized vocabulary. However, they are confident of meeting and overcoming the challenges (*attitude*), and are aware that new meanings will be revealed on further readings. Readers at this stage understand the benefits of focusing on details of print only when meaning has been lost (*understanding*). This is demonstrated in the way they adjust their reading pace to accommodate the purpose, style, form, and difficulty of the material. Readers at the fluency stage are able to maintain meaning over longer and more complex structures, and to respond to the author's message in a variety of ways (*behavior*).

Once the teacher is familiar with the children's interest and attitudes to reading, their understandings about books and the reader's role, and the observable ways in which they gain meaning from text, it is possible to select material that will motivate and support further development. This is especially the case through the guided reading of texts that provide plenty of support but, at the same time, offer sufficient challenge to extend the reader's competence.

Publishers, consultants, and colleagues can make recommendations about the suitability of material, but it is the teacher's day-by-day observation and interaction with the children and the regular monitoring of their progress that should guide the selection. The following suggestions of desirable features in books for use at each of the three main stages should be considered alongside all that the teacher knows about each child's interest, competencies, and experiences.

Emergent Stage Guided Reading

Books for guided reading at the emergent stage need to have a story line strong enough to help beginning readers work toward gaining the author's intended meaning, rather than focusing on individual words. There should be a close match of text and picture, a gradual introduction of difficulties, and sufficient repetitive elements to enable children to find support in the book and to develop understandings about the constancy of print. The book should not expect the reader to cope with too many changes of scene, time, or incident. The book's layout should encourage the use of correct directionality skills, leading the reader through the text without confusion.

Early Level Guided Reading

Books for guided reading at the early level should reflect the children's widening experiences and their ability to cope with material portraying credible experiences of others. The match between text and illustration may not be so precise, with readers sometimes being required to add to or select from the information provided in the pictures. However, readers at this stage still rely on illustrations for prediction, as well as making increasing use of them for confirming their considered guesses about the author's ideas. Books for guided reading at this stage should encourage the reader to increase the number of cues used to search for, check, and maintain meaning. There will probably be less repetition (or the repetition will be of longer patterns) and more complex ideas than in books used at the emergent stage.

Fluency Stage Guided Reading

At the fluency stage books used for guided reading lead the reader beyond the text in varied ways. The books encourage readers to make more connections with books of similar content, style, or form. They also present longer and more complex plots, and require the reader to cope with more characters, time changes, incidents, and alternatives within the story. Illustrations often reflect mood rather than action; and they complement rather than mirror the story. The more specialized vocabulary and the breadth of curriculum areas included increases at this level.

The type and form of material used at any level should exceed that expected in the children's directed and undirected writing. At each stage guided reading enables the teacher to show children unique features of form and style, not only to help them as they read the text of others but when they are creating their own.

GUIDED READING GROUP

Guided reading is most successful when the teacher can spend fifteen to twenty minutes with a small group of children who each have a copy of the same book. The teacher and children should be able to think and talk and read without being distracted by, or disturbing, the rest of the children, who will probably be engrossed in other reading and writing. The guided reading group could gather on part of the carpet area or around a small table. It is important that the children are comfortable and able to interact easily with one another and with the teacher. Neither the teacher nor the children should feel frustrated by time restrictions. Most teachers find spending time with two separate groups for guided reading each day allows sufficient time for other reading and writing activities, for responding to individual children, and for some regular monitoring and assessment.

Sample Lesson: Guided Reading at The Early Stage[1]

NICK'S GLASSES [2]

Nick's Glasses is suitable for guided reading with children who are gaining confidence in taking risks and making approximations, and who are using graphophonic cues for confirmation. The book encourages children to use these cues as the match of text and illustration is inconsistent.

Each child in the group of no more than eight should have a copy of the book. The children will already have had many guided reading experiences, so they will be aware of their role in the first reading of the book. The teacher could then introduce *Nick's Glasses* and help the children to set their purpose for reading by asking or suggesting:

What's the title?

---

[1] See Chapter 3 for a discussion of the early stage.
[2] Cachemaille, Christine. *Nick's Glasses*, in Ready to Read series. Wellington, New Zealand: Department of Education, 1982. Distributed in the United States by Richard C. Owen Publishers, Inc.

What does the cover tell you about Nick?
What questions do you expect the book to answer?

Title Page

Look at the title page.
What does this tell you about the story you have in your head?

Page 2

The illustrator takes the reader into her confidence by showing Nick wearing his glasses. None of the characters look directly at Nick until page 7. This trust in the reader is continued in the questions in the text, none of which are answered until the last page.

Read page 2 to discover Nick's problem.
Whom do you think Nick will ask for help?
Where do you think they will tell Nick to look?
Keep those ideas in your head. They will help you as you
read the story.

Page 3

·Read page 3 to find out where Mum told Nick to look.
How do you know you were right? or How did you check
you were right?

If a child replies that the picture says so, the teacher
could encourage attention to using the text to confirm predictions by saying:

"Where are my glasses?"
said Nick.

"Have you looked
under your bed?"
said Mum.

How did you check in the text that you were right?
Which words told you so?
Can you show me those words?

The reading could continue with:

Who else could Nick ask?
Turn the page to find out if you were right.

Page 4

Where did Dad tell Nick to look?
Which words told you that?
How did you check?
Tell your neighbor how you knew you were right.

"Have you looked
in your school bag?"
said Dad.

"Have you looked
on the table?"
said Jane.

Page 5

Read page 5 with your eyes.
Why is Nick looking under the table?

Some children may say that Jane told Nick to do so. This will indicate that they are still relying on picture clues, and they will need to have more specific questions asked to encourage them to look for more help in the text. The teacher could ask:

Which part of the text told you that?
How did you check it?
What letter does the word start with?
Can you hear that letter at the beginning of your guess?

"Have you looked behind the TV?" said Peter.

"Have you looked in the mirror?"

Because some children could think that "under" and "on" have a similar initial sound they may need to be guided to look at the word endings also.

What do you think now?

Page 6

What was Peter's question?

The picture on this page does not provide any confirmation, and graphophonic cues will probably be the main check.

What happened when Nick looked in the mirror?
What do you think Nick said?
Turn to the next page to see if you were right.

"Oh!" said Nick.
"Here they are!"

Questions following the reading could include:

How do you think Nick felt and what do you think he said when he realized he was already wearing his glasses?
Have you ever searched for something that you already had, so it was not lost after all?
How did you feel?

Before the children move on to another activity they should have an opportunity to reread the book by themselves or with one of the group members. Or they may just choose to browse through the book, view the illustrations, or talk about some aspects of the book with one of their peers or the teacher. The main thing is that the children are not immediately directed to a predetermined activity which checks whether or not the meaning gained by readers concurred with that expected by the teacher. They need time to absorb the story and to assimilate it into their own experience and understanding.

Sample Lesson: Guided Reading at The Fluency Stage[1]

THE GREAT GRUMBLER AND THE WONDER TREE[2]

The Great Grumbler and the Wonder Tree is suitable for guided reading by children working at the upper levels of the fluency stage who are able to make inferences from text as well as illustrations. The book provides opportunities for readers to take a more active part in interacting with the author's ideas and style in order to understand more complex characters. Questions asked during the reading should lead to conjecture and encourage more critical reading of longer passages in order to answer a question. As with all guided reading sessions each child should have a copy of the book and should be eager to assume the reader's role on the first reading.

[1] See Chapter 3 for a discussion of the fluency stage.
[2] Mahy, Margaret. *The Great Grumbler and the Wonder Tree,* in Ready to Read series. Wellington, New Zealand: Department of Education, 1984. Distributed in the United States by Richard C. Owen Publishers, Inc.

Discussion of the front cover and the title page should stimulate ideas that will help the children formulate their own purpose for the reading. Further questions should help children clarify and achieve their purpose without introducing too many other issues.

> Open the book so that you can see both covers.
> You'll be able to see all of the characters in the book.
> What conversation do you think is taking place on the front cover?
> And on the back cover?
> What's taken place in between?
> What kind of story do you think it's going to be?

It is important that any discussion in response to these questions does not focus on or reveal details of the story line, or there will be no reason for children to put any effort into taking responsibility or controlling the first reading.

Title Page

> A witch on a garden fork?
> Where do you think she's going?
> Why?

Page 2

> Read the text on this page to find out who has a problem.
> What is the problem?
> If you were the author how would you solve it?

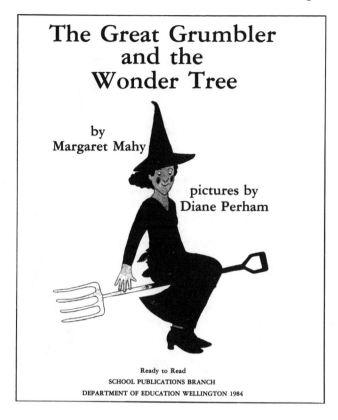

The Great Grumbler
and the
Wonder Tree

by
Margaret Mahy

pictures by
Diane Perham

Ready to Read
SCHOOL PUBLICATIONS BRANCH
DEPARTMENT OF EDUCATION WELLINGTON 1984

Questions during the reading should carry the story line forward and help readers to "get inside" the characters. For example:

How do you think Mr. Finch will be satisfied?
What would you do if you were Mrs. Finch?
What else could Mr. Finch complain about?

At this level the children should be able to discuss and set their own questions and goals within the reading. For example:

Read on until there's a new episode or a change in the plot.

Or,

Let's read the next two pages by ourselves before we share ideas.

Mrs Finch went to Gretel, the garden witch.
"My husband is a great grumbler,"
she said.
"Nothing I grow is good enough for him."

"I'll give you a seed
which will settle that," said Gretel.
"It is hard to grow,
but you are a good gardener.
It's the seed of the wonder tree.
Mind you, it's not free.
You will have to pay me
with a trailer-load of turnips."

"Right!" said Mrs Finch.
"I'll bring them over with my tractor
at two o'clock this afternoon."

3

Questions at the end of the reading could consider the author's style:

Why do you think Margaret Mahy wrote this idea in this style and form?
How would you have written it?
What changes would you make to the story line?
To the characters?
To the illustrations?

The lesson could end with the children being introduced to other books by Margaret Mahy or talking about those already familiar to them. The children should know where to get access to the books and be confident that the teacher will be interested in their voluntary responses.

9

Independent Reading

Independent reading—reading by children—is an approach to be nurtured at every stage of children's reading development. This is in direct contrast to many earlier understandings about reading and teaching practices, where independence was considered to be an observable stage marking a decrease in the amount of teaching necessary. Independence was seen as a magical moment before which children weren't considered to be capable of reading on their own, but after which they were expected to be able to read everything.

Independence as an integral part of every stage acknowledges the developmental nature of learning and the importance of new learning being grounded in and supported by the learning which has already taken place. It also means that from their earliest days children know that others believe they can read; they choose to read; they know how to make time to read; and they are encouraged to do so. Children have time for reading, space to enjoy reading in comfort and peace, and a variety of materials from which they can choose.

There will be more independent reading at the later stages of children's development, but the approach should be an integral part of the daily program of every class, even kindergarten. Providing for independent reading at every stage acknowledges children as achievers as well as learners, and allows children to confirm as well as extend their roles as readers and writers. Reading independently provides opportunities for children to rehearse and refine the attitudes, understandings, and behaviors they gained from models of stories that have been read to them and the approximations they have been encouraged to make in shared and guided reading.

Independent reading is a complement to the other approaches. In "reading to" children are motivated to be readers and writers; in shared reading and language experience that desire becomes a reality, as the children are co-readers and co-writers; and in guided reading children are able to prove to themselves that they have the resources to be successful readers and writers. In independent reading children assume the responsibility and control that has been developed through these more supportive approaches.

TEACHER'S ROLE

The teacher's role changes from one of initiating, modeling, and guiding to one of providing and then observing, acknowledging, and responding. Figure 2.1 shows how the balance of support and responsibility varies from approach to approach. However, the teacher does not abdicate all responsibility during independent reading. Children need to know that the teacher is interested in their reading and their responses to the reading. The teacher uses the time to observe the way children initiate and sustain their independent reading experiences.

BOOKS FOR INDEPENDENT READING

Books available for independent reading should include all those which have been read to the children and used in shared and guided reading. There should also be plenty of books which the children have chosen themselves (perhaps including some from the school library), as well as a wide variety of as-yet-unseen books which the teacher has gathered from all available sources. These books should not present too many difficulties for children as they enjoy browsing through them and reading most of them successfully.

Books available for independent reading should reflect a balance between favorites, books at the children's current level, some which have been introduced recently, and some new titles. The books should vary in type, form, and style, and the content should reflect the children's interests as well as the classroom curriculum. The stock of books, or part of it, should be changed regularly, with children taking part in the sifting and sorting process as well as in the selecting of new titles. In this way children learn how to identify favorite books, to view a range of new ones, and to select those they are eager to explore next. The children can also "sell" their favorite books to other children, and to share reactions to individual books as well as to authors or types of books.

This shared process of restocking enables the teacher to identify those books which are favorites with individuals as well as the majority of children; and to establish why they are popular, as well as discuss with the children the books they have forgotten or passed over.

Part of the teacher's role in independent reading is to find, offer, and introduce books to readers. And part of the readers' role is to know how to choose books which will satisfy their current abilities and interests.

BOOK CORNER

The books should be displayed in a well-lit and easily accessible part of the classroom, although the area should not be in the path of the main traffic flow where children would be frequently distracted or disturbed. The book corner should be inviting for children. There should be room for them to sit and read alone or with others. Readers who treasure books take care of them, and the teacher should share this responsibility with the children. If children are to take care of books and consider them a pleasurable and worthwhile part of their lives, they need to see the teacher valuing books.

TIME TO READ

One way in which teachers can show they value reading as an enjoyable habit and want the children to experience the successes and pleasures of reading for themselves is by making time available each day for independent reading. The teacher needs to be seen to be reading for his or her own enjoyment as well as allowing the children time and freedom to read for their pleasure. Reading without being required to share is an important part of a daily program.

Children should have access to the book corner at all times. There will be occasions when the teacher will suggest that the children read, and times when a book is recommended or the children are asked to read it; but these times should be balanced by many opportunities for the children to initiate their own reading. Knowing that one can read, and being able to choose to do so, is a habit that should be established early and nurtured continuously.

10

Continuing the Dialogue

POSITIVE FEELINGS

Whatever approach has been used, children should finish the reading feeling satisfied with their efforts, motivated to continue the dialogue with the author, and expectant that future reading experiences will be as enjoyable as this one. These positive feelings about their roles as creator and recreator of meaning will be enhanced if the children are able to act as real readers and writers in the post-reading phase. Children should be given many opportunities to revisit texts on their own, and to explore new books or to choose to follow other responses engendered by the reading experience. The focus should remain on the children and on them confirming, refining, and extending their learning. That means some of the responsibility and control must be maintained by the readers themselves.

This is in direct contrast to traditional practices where, prior to the reading, teachers have determined which tasks will be appropriate for the post-reading period. The focus is then on the teacher's agenda, and on instructing and teaching or practice and checking. When children know that a reading is going to be followed by tasks assigned by the teacher, they lose the sense of ownership of meaning and, in time, they will not bother to actively engage in relating the author's ideas to their own experiences. Children's reading is manipulated by what they are going to need in order to complete the assignment and win the teacher's approval.

No two children will acquire exactly the same message or feeling from any reading, and the unanswered questions will differ from child to child and from book to book for any one child. The traditional pattern of following a reading with a time of prepared activities (even if some choice is offered) does not necessarily help children to find acceptable answers, or make the story more memorable, or increase the readers' competence. If children are to associate reading with satisfaction, challenge and success, continued learning, and increased understanding about themselves and their world the post-reading phase needs to reflect these aspects in a personal way.

The reading of a story may remind some children of another they have read previously; and they may wish to reread and make a response to that book. For some children the reading may have sparked their imaginations in a completely different direction. They will remain preoccupied with these new thoughts for some time, and no set assignment will satisfy their needs or distract them from their own thoughts. Others may have found it difficult to make a real connection with the author, and so they do not wish to pursue the reading any further. Some of these children may return to the story later, but others will have no inclination to do so. Still other children may already be concentrating on, or trying to complete, another task.

HELP WITH POST-READING TASKS

A few children may not know what they want to do; and the teacher will need to offer guidance by suggesting some options within the children's capabilities. However, this group is similar to all others—the desire to continue dialogue with the author, and the way in which they wish to do so, should be to further each reader's understanding and enjoyment, and not to meet the teacher's checklist or publisher's teaching sequence.

To, with, and by should be features of the post-reading time as well as of the actual reading. It is a time for learning, not testing. The models and support which helped children to exchange meaning through talk and to engage with the author through a book need to be in place following the reading. Only then will children be able to respond freely and go beyond a superficial skim.

In the same way that children need to be shown how to initiate some reading and to control the input, they need to be shown how to decide whether or not to make a response after the reading and, if so, how. The teacher will need to explore the options with children and help them make an appropriate choice. Children can only make a wise choice when they know what they are choosing not to select.

This does not mean that every child in the class or group will always be working on different tasks. But it may require the teacher to change from relying on predetermined or prepared activities to thinking through the children's ideas with them as they try to make a choice and then collectively decide what is manageable.

Some children may wish to work alone. Others may choose to work in a small group; while others will be eager to be one of a larger group working on a common task. This should differ from time to time for any child; and the teacher will need to watch for any children who always or never want to work alone.

The teacher also needs to be aware of children who never vary their responses to a text, either in content or form. It may be that these children lack confidence to explore new directions, fearing less-than-perfect results; or they may feel insecure about the acceptance of their efforts by their peers. In these cases the teacher would need to consider the nature of support given to the children and ways in which they could be encouraged to be more accepting of the ideas and efforts of others. A nonthreatening and accepting, yet challenging, environment is essential for continuous and natural learning.

There should be a balance of demonstration and direction in the content and form of responses. If the children are to be expected and trusted to initiate and follow through their own responses, the principle of to, with, and by needs to be reflected in the way any one topic is explored in many different forms, as well as many topics in any one form. For example, following the reading of "Pita's Birthday"[1] the teacher and children could discuss the different ways they could choose to share their memories of their last birthdays. These responses could include stories, picture sequences, a replica of an invitation to the party or one of the cards received, a list of those who attended the party or the presents received, a play about the party or a dramatization of the making of the cake or of opening the presents, a replica of the menu, a poem about waking up on the morning of the birthday, a diary entry for the birthday, an adaptation or extra verses for a birthday song, thank-you letters, or a book of birthday greetings in several languages (especially those known to children in the class). Or, the teacher and children could explore a form or type of writing. For example, talking about the ways to record the event in a diary or making lists.

The teacher can help children to think through their choices and to take responsibility for these by asking questions that will take them beyond the initial "I want to . . ." These questions could include a selection of the following:

Why did you make that choice?
What will you need?
Do you know where you will get it?
How much time will you need?
If you don't finish it today, will you be able to continue it tomorrow?
Are you going to work alone or with . . . ?
If you need help, whom will you ask? When?

[1] Cowley, Joy. "Pita's Birthday" in *Pita's Birthday*, Ready to Read series. Wellington, New Zealand: Department of Education, 1985. Distributed in the United States by Richard C. Owen Publishers, Inc.

What will you do when you finish?
Do you think you will want to share your work with someone/me/the class?

The children should not be bombarded with all of these questions at any one time. If the selection varies from time to time the children will respond more thoughtfully. During the first months at school and the first days in a new classroom the teacher and children explore the options in their answers, but once routines are established and the children are familiar with the layout of the room and the resources available the questions become guides for thought rather than requests for answers.

TIME AND RESOURCES

Children cannot be responsible for the management of their time and effort unless they have easy and continued access to resources beyond those normally kept in their cubbyholes, totes, or desks. They need to know where to find and how to use and return items such as glue, scissors, staplers, wool, string, paper and cards of all shapes and sizes, collage materials, dressup materials, the listening post, the overhead projector, construction materials, and as many quality books as possible.

Access to resources needs to be accompanied by space in which to use them. Classroom walls cannot be extended, but the contents can be rearranged so that children can move around the room freely without disturbing those occupied in other tasks. Many resource books include room plans. These can be helpful guides; but the unique features of each room; the number and age, and the interests and abilities of the children; the teacher's style of working; and the program content will dictate the most functional arrangement of each room. As any of these factors change, so will the room arrangement; and the children will need to reorient themselves to where the various resources can now be found.

Access to reasonable blocks of time is also a requirement if children are to follow through with their choices and make responses more than a superficial dash. Continued and realistic appraisal of the children's collective and individual capabilities and available resources will help ensure that children are able to set and meet their goals. If the language period is fragmented into too many small tasks the children will be overwhelmed and daunted by the number of these to be accomplished and frustrated by those left unfinished. As the children make more connections with authors and among books of similar form, theme, and type, they will become dissatisfied with their efforts if they are unable to work in depth. Yet children should not be left for long spans of time where they are unsupported or where resources are insufficient to add variety or meet expectations or demands.

Providing reasonable blocks of time does not mean that the teacher leaves the children to their own devices. The teacher's role becomes one of respondent and interested observer, interceding when support is sought or is necessary for the work to be completed without too much frustration or disturbance to the rest of the class. The children are aware of the teacher's watchful and supportive eye; but the incentive to accomplish the task is the reward of the task itself and not solely to earn the teacher's praise.

11

Sharing the Responses

Many of the responses to text remain within the reader or are shared with the teacher, another child, or a small group. Other responses can be shared with the whole class. Some of these responses do not lend themselves to permanency, although they may have significance for the initiator for some time. The effort expended in such responses, and their value as signs of assimilation of the author's message, should be acknowledged.

However, some of the children's responses can support and extend the learning of others by being displayed and used within the classroom. The classroom environment should reflect "to, with, and by" in the way the material is prepared and displayed, as well as in the way children use it to make further responses or respond to the work of others. The work displayed should be motivated by guided and independent reading experiences, as well as those experiences stimulated by being read to or participating in shared reading.

DISPLAYS

A display should invite children to read and respond to the work of others and encourage them to contribute some of their own. The work should continue to be part of the program and not just a finale or decoration, and most of the work should be the children's. It is the children who are the reason for the existence of the classroom. It is their efforts, experiences, and interests which should be acknowledged and valued.

When work is displayed so children can view it and, where possible, touch it, the display itself can be the spark for further learning. The children can add their responses to the work of others; and the teacher and children can discuss and read and react together. These reactions do not have to be instant, although work should not remain on display once it holds no further interest or becomes ragged. Any work displayed should be revisited frequently for, as with all quality stories and work, new meanings will be revealed and appreciations heightened on subsequent readings. Sometimes the revisiting will take place during a directed or undirected "group time" or with and by individual children; but it could also be part of class time at the commencement or end of a period, or as a "break" during the day.

Sometimes, questions inviting further responses could be posed by the teacher or included in the display. Cards seeking responses could be placed near or below the display. These questions or suggestions could include:

- Can you suggest another title or caption for this display?
- What is going to happen next? Write your ideas here.
- Can you add something to the display?
- Add a speech bubble to your favorite character telling what he/she is saying.
- Which character would you like to be? Why? Write your reason here.
- If you have any questions about this work, or the book it tells about, talk with _____ or _____.

Captions or books displayed nearby could lead the children back to the original publication or to further related reading. There could also be some indication of children who have other related work to share or are keen to discuss the book or read it to or with someone.

Making displays a working resource adds purpose to the children's responses, rewards their efforts in preparing them, and acknowledges the ideas as being worthy of consideration by others. It also enables children to enjoy and learn from the work of others.

12

Keeping Learning Alive

The approaches of "to, with, and by" promoted in this book emphasize the teacher's role in being more concerned with fostering learning than with teaching. It is suggested that the reason for presenting material in a particular way is to support the learning opportunities it will offer children. This means the teacher's decision making is driven by what children need for their learning rather than what children need to learn. The difference lies in the perception of the learner's role, with the former seeing the children actively involved in, and responsible for, much of their learning. Decisions based on what children need to learn put learners in the passive position of being controlled and merely the recipients and storers of knowledge.

Chapter 3, "Focusing on the Reader," outlined the importance of knowing the children's current stage of reading development as reflected in observable attitudes, understandings, and behaviors before being able to plan appropriate learning opportunities. Subsequent chapters have emphasized the need for the teacher to continually observe the children's reactions and their efforts in initiating, sustaining, and completing reading and writing tasks. In this way evaluation is an integral part of a program, with responsive teaching replacing the rather spasmodic examination of test results and children's "best" work.

Responsive teaching means the teacher is supporting the children, ensuring that their learning path is free of obstructions, and clarifying and illuminating their goals so they can frequently enjoy the success and rewards of achievement. Each achievement creates its own momentum for further learning. The children's development becomes a rhythm of success, new visions and starting points, experience and effort resulting in success and new visions. This pattern is occurring in many areas at any one time, so the feeling of achievement and moving forward is always with the child.

The responsive teacher experiences the same rhythm; and his or her tasks become rewarding in the same continuous and satisfying way. The children and teacher become models and respondents for each other, and so a learning community is born and nurtured, and living and learning become one.

13

A Child's View of Learning

Joy Cowley's *Greedy Cat*[1] had become one of Nathan's favorite books. Each day he returned to the book with renewed interest, reading it alone and then to a classmate. After several days Nathan decided to write his own "Greedy Cat" story. Nathan's story reflected his familiarity with the story line and language pattern of the original, although the spelling was definitely his own. He showed it to his teacher who responded, "That's great, Nathan. Have you finished?"

[1]Cowley, Joy, *Greedy Cat*, in Ready to Read series. Wellington, New Zealand: Department of Education, 1983. Distributed in the United States by Richard C. Owen Publishers, Inc.

Nathan looked slightly confused. He didn't appear to know what was expected. However, he took his paper back to the table, smiled, and quickly added, "By Nathan." He started to take the story back to the teacher but stopped, thought for a moment, hurried to the book corner, and found a copy of *Greedy Cat.* Nathan grabbed a pencil from a nearby table and added "and Joy Cowley" to his name in the author credit.

When he again showed his work to the teacher, Nathan pointed to "By Nathan and Joy Cowley," smiled the widest possible smile, and said, "I did most of it. She just helped me."